PRINTED IN U.S.A.

What Does a
CITIZEN
Do?

What Does a Protester Do?

PYLE

Enslow Publishing
101 W. 23rd Street
Suite 240
New York, NY 10011
USA

enslow.com

Bridey Heing

Published in 2019 by Enslow Publishing, LLC.
101 W. 23rd Street, Suite 240, New York, NY 10011

Library of Congress Cataloging-in-Publication Data

Names: Heing, Bridey, author.
Title: What does a protester do? / Bridey Heing.
Description: New York : Enslow Publishing, [2019] | Series: What does a
    citizen do? | Audience: Grade level 5-8. | Includes bibliographical
    references and index.
Identifiers: LCCN 2017058061| ISBN 9780766098725 (library bound) | ISBN
    9780766098732 (pbk.)
Subjects: LCSH: Protest movements—United States—Juvenile literature.
Classification: LCC HN59.2 .H45 2018 | DDC 303.48/40973—dc23
LC record available at https://lccn.loc.gov/2017058061

Printed in the United States of America

To Our Readers: We have done our best to make sure all website addresses in this book were active and appropriate when we went to press. However, the author and the publisher have no control over and assume no liability for the material available on those websites or on any websites they may link to. Any comments or suggestions can be sent by e-mail to customerservice@enslow.com.

Photo Credits: Cover, p. 1 Ken Wolter/Shutterstock.com; p. 4 BluIz60/Shutterstock.com; p. 9 Time Life Pictures/The LIFE Picture Collection/Getty Images; p. 12 Jack R Perry Photography/Shutterstock.com; pp. 15, 17, 19 Bettmann/Getty Images; p. 23 David McNew/Getty Images; p. 25 UfaBizPhoto/Shutterstock.com; p. 28 Justin Sullivan/Getty Images; p. 30 Bill Pugliano/Getty Images; p. 32 Sean Rayford/Getty Images; pp. 34–35 Boston Globe/Getty Images; pp. 36–37 Bill Eppridge/The LIFE Picture Collection/Getty Images; p. 41 Tim Sloan/AFP/Getty Images; pp. 42–43 NurPhoto/Getty Images.

CONTENTS

Protest is not only an American citizen's right, it's also essentially how the country was founded.

Introduction

Since the country's founding, protesters have played an important role in shaping the United States' culture, politics, and values. In fact, in many ways our country's story starts with protest; the United States gained independence from Great Britain in part as an act of protest against unfair governance. That relationship between the people and the state—a relationship built in part on the right to speak out against injustice or wrongdoing on the part of the government—is a key part of what makes the United States the country that it is. Protest is the cornerstone on which American democracy rests.

The right to assemble is one of the rights guaranteed by the First Amendment, and historically this has been upheld as enshrining the right to protest. As we'll see, it's not always that simple—there are restrictions on when and where formal protests can be held, and the Supreme Court has ruled that these restrictions do not infringe on the civil rights of citizens. Despite some limitations imposed by law, protests are most often considered a free speech issue, with the freedom of making their voices heard one of the rights protesters have relied on to keep them safe while gathering.

What Does a Protester Do?

Protest can take many forms, but most protests are organized by activists and community organizers using their own networks, the media, and increasingly social media sites like Twitter and Facebook. Marches are one of the most widely recognized forms of protest, but petitions, sit-ins, and rallies are also public displays of support for causes or shows of opposition. Counterprotests are also common, in which a public protest gives rise to a parallel protest meant to undermine the message of the original protest. All of these are rooted in the same drive—to make the voices of the people heard in order to effect change.

But protest can also be controversial; often centered on young people and challenging the status quo, protests can be lightning rods in society. Whether marching against wars or holding sit-ins against racial injustice, protests throughout American history have often been met with widespread condemnation before being seen as the historical moments of change we know them as today. In the past, protests have been met with outcry and violence, including instances in which protesters have been killed by police or others. Although a time-honored tradition, protests can be dangerous, with many people actively seeking to silence the voices of those who speak out.

Today, protests remain highly controversial, and the way we engage with protest is changing rapidly, causing some to question the role of protest in the twenty-first century. The rise of social media has lead to concerns that protest is becoming an online hobby rather than an in-the-streets action of radical, but civil, disobedience. But as we'll see, social media is a useful tool that can bring people from around the country—and the world—together to protest as one.

Protest has a complex place in American society, and protesters are on the forefront of guarding democracy through civic action. As we'll learn, the history of protest in America is the history of the country itself, from the earliest days of our history through the civil rights era and into today. Protest remains radical and controversial for the simple reason that it is an important facet of democracy and because protesters work hard to ensure the government serves all Americans.

Protest in US History

Today, protesters take to the streets, to town halls, and to online venues in order to make their voices heard on a number of issues. These actions are controversial, but they harken back to the very beginning of our country. The United States was born out of radical protest against a lack of representation in government, and that sense of the government being beholden to the governed was put into the Constitution. Since then, groups willing to raise their voices against injustice have been on the forefront of shaping the country and pushing us forward as a society by ensuring the rights of all Americans, voicing discontent with war, and seeking a better future.

The Beginning of a Nation

Protest is, in many ways, the very foundation of our country; if it hadn't been for citizens willing to stand up to those in power, the American Experiment never would have gotten started. Acts of protest were common in the colonies in the mid- to late 1700s.

Burning the Stamps.

American colonists were outraged by the Stamp Act, which imposed a British tax on printed material, spurring protests that demanded there be no taxation on colonists without representation in government.

What Does a Protester Do?

Actions ranged from simply disregarding British laws to developing widespread disruptions, as happened with the Stamp Act of 1765.

The Stamp Act was passed by the British in 1765 and imposed a tax on all printed materials in the colonies by requiring them to be made with special paper stamped to indicate a tax had been paid. Opposition to the act was based on the belief that the British had no right to impose taxes on the colonies without the permission of colonial authorities, an argument that gave rise to the slogan "No taxation without representation." Anger was so widespread that the Stamp Act Congress was formed, bringing together representatives from all the colonies to petition the British government. This sense of unity was important; it was the first time the colonies worked together to protest a measure by the British, and it established links between merchants, landowners, and leaders.

Average citizens were also active in voicing their dissent. The Sons of Liberty, a group that included John Hancock, Patrick Henry, Paul Revere, and others, was founded at this time to organize protests and intimidate those who might adhere to the tax. Through their actions, which were sometimes violent, the tax was never able to be collected. Although the group itself was likely disbanded, members would go on to play an active role in the revolution that followed a decade later.

One of the most famous protests in American history took place in 1773, just three years before independence was declared and the American Revolution began. The Boston Tea Party was launched by the Sons of Liberty in response to the Tea Act of 1773. That act was another attempt by the British to impose taxes on the colonies, this time imposing a three pence duty on tea imported to the colonies.

The Boston Tea Party was one of several protests against the Tea Act. In other colonies, protesters were able to force shipments of tea to turn around before landing, effectively refusing to pay for the imported tea. But in Boston they were unable to gain support from local authorities, and the ships were able to land in port. In response, men dressed as Native Americans boarded the three ships that made port in Boston and threw more than three hundred chests of tea into the water.

The Boston Tea Party was one catalyst for a wave of change that swept the colonies, bringing about the First Continental Congress, organized resistance to the British, and eventually the American Revolution. Disobedience to unjust laws was what brought activists and leaders together across the colonies and created the environment needed to assert independence, and it all started with protest.

Enshrining the Right to Be Heard

Given the important role of protest in beginning the American Experiment, it is no surprise that civil assembly was considered an important cornerstone of the new government. The Founders considered it crucial that citizens have means by which they could petition the government and make their voices heard, and protest was an important part of that. As such, they built these rights into the Bill of Rights.

The First Amendment includes some of our most treasured rights, including the right to free speech and freedom of the press. It also include the "right peaceably to assembly" and the "right to petition for a governmental redress of grievances." Both of these play a role in ensuring the right to protest as we know it today.

The First Amendment, which includes the right to peaceably assemble and the right to petition the government, guarantees that US citizens have the right to protest.

The right to assembly ensures the right of citizens to congregate in order to pursue or make heard their ideals. This could include people holding a rally or people holding a private meeting. It does not guarantee the right to assemble anywhere; people protesting on public land need to have a permit or the permission of the owner to protest on private land. It is also important to note the caveat of "peaceably," indicating that violent protest, such as riots, will not be tolerated by the state. The police can also end protests or rallies that are seen as a threat to public health and safety, such as those blocking roads or deviating from their permit in a way that could do harm.

The right to petition government for redress of grievances is perhaps a trickier one to understand on first read, but it is just as important. The impact of this constitutional right is simple: it gives citizens the right to complain to their government and has been an important basic civil right since the Magna Carta. By ensuring the right to petition one's government, citizens are able to make their concerns heard directly to their government and legislators without fear of reprisal. While this does not mean that each complaint will be handled directly, it does mean that protesters are able to express themselves clearly without concern.

Shaping the United States Through Protest

Since the late 1700s, protest has driven change and reform in the United States. Almost all movements that expanded citizenship, inclusion, and rights began as popular protests organized by a dedicated core of people who went above and beyond to make their voices heard. Below are just a few of the protest movements that have shaped our country through mass action.

Abolition

Although slavery formally ended following the Civil War, prior to that abolitionists protested the continued practice of slavery in the United States. Quakers were among the first to organize societies devoted to the dismantling of slavery, organizing petitions, boycotts, and public speeches against the institution. Others, both black and white, advocated for the banning of the slave trade or argued that Christian values and slavery were incompatible. Sojourner Truth, a woman born into slavery who later became one of the most outspoken abolitionists, was one woman of color who traveled the country agitating against slavery. Harriet Tubman was another woman of color who established the underground railroad, the secret network of safe houses that gave passage for slaves from the South to the North, where slavery was already outlawed. This act was a form of protest and disobedience, an important way to undermine slavery ahead of full abolition.

Suffrage

In the late 1800s, the women's suffrage movement gained significant attention as protests were mounted around the country. The Seneca Falls Convention of 1848 is, in many ways, where the movement gained momentum, although women had been calling for the right to vote since the founding of the United States. Leaders like Elizabeth Cady Stanton, Lucretia Mott, Susan B. Anthony, and Ida B. Wells were among those who launched campaigns, wrote articles, started marches, and even endured time in prison to secure the right to vote for women. Hunger strikes were carried out by those who were arrested, and often they were faced with forced feedings

In 1838, at the age of twenty, Frederick Douglass escaped slavery by traveling to the free state of New York. He went on to become a famous abolitionist and writer.

Cesar Chavez

Protests have historically been conducted on behalf of marginalized populations, often those who are under threat or are underrepresented in power. Cesar Chavez is one organizer who, along with others like Dolores Huerta, raised the issue of such a population: farm workers. A former farm worker himself, he and Huerta founded the National Farm Worker's Association, which became the United Farm Workers union. Along with other protesters, Chavez staged mass strikes, marches, and hunger strikes on behalf of the thousands of farm workers around the United States who were exploited by their lack of collective bargaining and regulated protections. His work helped secure higher wages and other protections for farm workers and made him an icon of civil rights. In the late 1960s, he also became allied with Robert Kennedy, and following Kennedy's assassination in 1968, Kennedy's widow, Ethel, continued the family's work with Chavez. Today, he and Huerta are considered as leaders of nonviolent protest in the United States and are honored around the country. Although Chavez passed away in 1993, Huerta remains an active campaigner for labor and civil rights.

Passed in 1920, the Nineteenth Amendment finally granted women the right to vote, but only after many decades of protests. Even though the law included all women, it was still difficult for women of color to vote.

by authorities. It took until 1920, after decades of women being arrested, beaten, and attacked in the media, for the Nineteenth Amendment to be passed and for women to gain the right to vote, and it took even longer for women of color to be able to vote safely.

Civil Rights

Following the abolition of slavery, a great deal of prejudice still existed in the United States, which made itself manifest through laws, societies aimed at intimidating communities of color, and other institutionalized forms of racism with which the United States still struggles today. In the 1950s and 1960s, leaders in the African American community organized protests aimed at challenging obstruction of their right to vote, Jim Crow laws in states and cities across the country, and continued verbal and violent harassment of their communities by groups like the KKK. Leaders like Martin Luther King Jr., Marcus Garvey, and Malcolm X organized protests and actions across the country, including the famous Montgomery Bus Boycott and the March on Washington. Their actions secured the Voting Rights Act of 1965, which barred states from implementing laws that would restrict access to the polls and kick-started conversations around race in America. But Martin Luther King Jr. and Malcolm X, among others, were assassinated, underlining the dangers posed by doing the important work of standing up to injustice.

Vietnam War

The 1960s also saw the vast expansion of the Vietnam War, which began in 1955 and ended in 1975 when American forces were withdrawn from the nation. Protests against the war began in the 1960s, focused primarily on college campuses and in cities. The growing counterculture movement of that time, including the so called hippies, also carried out protests including marches, sit-ins, and rallies. Public anger over the war was based in the seemingly unjust war itself, the draft, and the long duration of the conflict. Iconography that remains popular, including the slogan "Make Love, Not War," came out of the antiwar movement, which included veterans, students, average citizens, and others. But the antiwar movement was also controversial, due in part to its association with cities,

The war in Vietnam was an unpopular one, and US involvement incited several protests, especially from college students.

beliefs like "free love," and drug usage. Even so, the antiwar protests sparked national conversations about the role of the military in American culture, the place of the United States around the world, and the importance of diplomacy over invasions.

LGBTQ+ Rights

The fight for LGBTQ+ rights stretches back centuries, but for most of human history homosexuality has been considered a crime or has been shunned by society. This began to change in 1969, when the Stonewall riots in New York City kick-started the growing LGBTQ+ rights movement. The Stonewall Inn was a famous LGBTQ+ club, and when police attempted to raid the bar on June 28, 1969, those who were there responded by rioting—a spontaneous protest that is now considered the foundation for the movement that has won legal protections and rights. Protests for LGBTQ+ rights would spread throughout the 1970s to encompass cities across the country, including San Francisco and Chicago. Although today the fight continues, major successes like securing the right to marry and nondiscrimination legislation have been done through the ceaseless work of organizers and allies in the LGBTQ+ community.

How Protests Are Organized

Protests are often thought of as passionate displays of values, ideals, or concerns. But a lot goes into making a protest a success; they don't just happen organically. In fact, it takes days and even weeks to organize a protest, depending on the location, size, and rules that apply in a certain area. Community organizers, law enforcement, and volunteers have to work together to make sure everyone is safe and that their voices are heard in the most effective way.

Bringing People Together

There are many kinds of protests that are organized around the country, from one-day events to online petitions to long-standing acts of resistance. But they all start in the same place: identifying a problem and rallying those who care about it. This is most often the job of a community organizer or similar professional who understands how to bring people together and is familiar with the regulations on protests, although it can be a volunteer or other person.

What Does a Protester Do?

Before organizing a protest, it is important to lay out the goals of the event and identify those who are interested in advocating for it. The goals for a protest can be vague, like raising awareness for an issue or showing solidarity for a cause. But they can also be very specific, such as changing a local law or challenging a governmental action. The organizer has to make clear these specific goals and any other parts of the platform for which people will be protesting; everyone who walks, signs, or otherwise participates has a right to know what they are supporting before they agree to do so.

The organizer also needs to find a way to bring people together around the cause for which they are advocating. They can do this in a few ways; word of mouth through their network or via social media are just two avenues for raising interest. Other organizations might also want to lend support, and an organizer might send out a press release that details the upcoming event in order to drum up more interest. At this point the organizer might also invite speakers who are leaders on the issue to address the crowd, or the organizer might plan on speaking themselves if the protest is smaller in scale.

These early steps are the most important; they lay the foundation for a successful protest. But they are only the beginning of a long process.

Abiding by the Law

Protests are meant to be inspiring and impactful, but they also have to be lawful. Once an organizer has a cause, it is important to learn about the regulations and rules for protests in the area where the protest will take place. This can include getting permits from the city, coordinating with law enforcement, or getting private security to ensure the safety of others. Checking on things like where

Depending on the laws of the city, permits that specify certain regulations, like where a protest can take place, are sometimes required.

marches can take place, what is required for a march to be lawful, or what kinds of clothing protesters can wear will help make sure the event goes smoothly.

Permits are often fairly straightforward, requiring a form and a fee to be paid to the city. But it is important to coordinate dates in regard to other events to ensure an area remains safe for those who are not taking part in the protest. A permit will also provide guidelines for times when the protest can take place, the route for

Protests and Social Media

Social media has completely changed the way protests are organized and, in some cases, carried out. This has caused debate and celebration, because while sites like Facebook make it possible to organize people very quickly, it can be harder to ensure turnout from those who commit to action online. Organizers can use Facebook pages or Twitter accounts to gauge interest in action, create events through which people around the world can organize, or circulate petitions to audiences who otherwise would never be able to find them. But there is a difference between signing up for an event on social media and actually showing up, and that gulf is something that organizers struggle to bridge. But in some cases, the opposite can happen. In 2017, the Women's March began as an offhand idea posted on a personal Facebook page, but it quickly grew to millions of people marching in cities around the world, all showing solidarity for women's rights. The march showed the power of social media, but also the difficulty in harnessing that potential effectively, as months of work were required to make the events happen in cities like Washington, DC; Los Angeles; New York; London; and Paris.

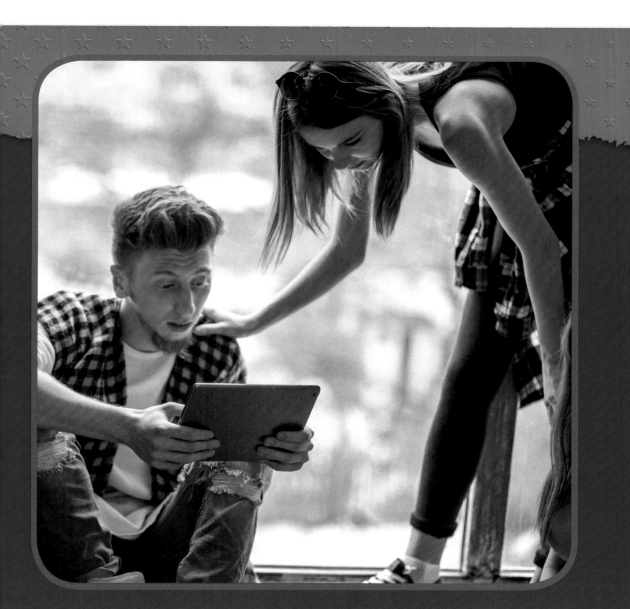

Social media has become a powerful tool for connecting like-minded activists and organizing protests.

any marching or movement of people, and expectations for orderly behavior.

Maintaining the lawful nature of the protest is crucial for safety and to make sure no one gets arrested. But it is also important that organizers plan for the worst, which can include working with the American Civil Liberties Union or the National Lawyers Guild to make sure observers are present to track any mistakes by either the protesters or the authorities. As we'll learn, even following the rules doesn't always ensure a protest isn't broken up or otherwise targeted by the police, and many of history's greatest leaders have been arrested for civil disobedience during protests—including Martin Luther King Jr. Although protest should always be carried out in accordance with local law, the relationship between power and protest has always been troubled, and it is important to remember this when the media or those in power try to dismiss protesters due to regulations.

Making Space for the Unexpected

Before a protest, the organizer should have a game plan for the event, permits, and an exact schedule. But no matter how well planned, protests sometimes take unexpected turn. This could include a sudden change in circumstances, such as a bill suddenly being withdrawn, or a logistical change, like more people showing up than anticipated. These sudden changes can be handled effectively by organizers if they build into their plan possible issues and work with law enforcement or the city to accommodate the changes.

It is also important for protesters themselves to be ready for anything. Wearing comfortable shoes and warm clothes in the winter or cool clothes in the summer makes long hours in the streets

High-profile speakers at protests can stir the crowd, building momentum for further action and activism.

easier to handle, and staying hydrated will reduce the chance of a medical emergency. Listening to leaders and being adaptable are also great ways to make sure the average protester does his or her part to keep things running smoothly.

At the same time, paying attention to the tone of the event can make the difference in staying safe; if people begin disrupting the event or if for any reason protesters feel unsafe, it is important that they alert one of the organizers and potentially leave the area.

What Does a Protester Do?

Protests are often targeted by law enforcement if people begin breaking the law, sometimes responding with pepper spray or rubber bullets. The safety of all protesters is the first and foremost concern for organizers, so speaking to someone leading the protest is a good way to find out about resources or a safety plan.

Capitalizing on Momentum

Following a successful protest, organizers have to make sure they do not let the energy of the cause slow down. Finding ways to keep the issue a topic of conversation or rallying supporters to take other actions is a way to maintain the momentum of a protest while making tangible gains for a cause. This could include organizing local petitions, identifying legislation on which supporters can contact their legislators, or putting together other community-based tasks. Protests are often a high-energy moment outside of normal life, but if they are to have a lasting impact the organizers have to find ways to make the cause on behalf of which the protest took place a focus moving forward.

Protecting the Right to Protest

Protest is a politically charged act that has great power to effect change. As a result, throughout history the right to protest has been challenged or even eroded. This can be through legal action, like withdrawing permits, or police action, including shootings or other violent means to intimidate or break up protests. The right to protest also intersects with other significant rights, like free speech, which results in complicated court cases that protect speech that many feel should not be lawful. Through all this, organizers and protesters continue to stand on the front lines of the fight for the right to protest.

The Police and Protest

The police play an important part in protests, ensuring that all remain safe and that any laws or regulations are followed closely. But police and other authorities can also pose a threat to protest, and in the past violence has broken out between protesters and the National Guard, local police, or other armed security forces. This complex

What Does a Protester Do?

Police officers often have to intervene to keep protests and counter-protests organized, lawful, and safe.

relationship can cause tension at even peaceful protests, with many fearing that a few people can cause a violent crackdown.

There are valid reasons why authorities break up protests. This can include damage to property or threats to the safety of others, as in a riot or other violent protest. But sometimes the police respond with undue force to unarmed protesters, causing death, injury, and a deep lack of trust between the communities they protect and the authorities.

One example of this is the Kent State shootings of May 1970. That day, protests against the Vietnam War had culminated in a gathering of a few thousands college students and other protesters. After days of similar protests, the National Guard had been called in to disperse the protests, which were characterized as violent and dangerous. The day before the shooting, the governor of Ohio said in a speech:

> We've seen here at the city of Kent especially, probably the most vicious form of campus-oriented violence yet perpetrated by dissident groups. They make definite plans of burning, destroying, and throwing rocks at police and at the National Guard and the Highway Patrol. This is when we're going to use every part of the law enforcement agency of Ohio to drive them out of Kent. We are going to eradicate the problem. We're not going to treat the symptoms. And these people just move from one campus to the other and terrorize the community. They're worse than the brown shirts and the communist element and also the night riders and the vigilantes. They're the worst type of people that we harbor in America. Now I want to say this. They are not going to take over [the] campus. I think that we're up against the strongest, well-trained, militant, revolutionary group that has ever assembled in America.[1]

Language like this is often used against protesters as a way to dismiss or undermine them, and it can have dangerous ramifications.

What Does a Protester Do?

At Kent State, on May 4, the National Guard attempted to break up the protests with tear gas, but protesters began throwing rocks and yelling abuse at the guardsmen. Shortly after noon, after advancing on the protesters, the National Guard opened fire on the unarmed demonstrators, shooting sixty-seven rounds and killing four university students. It was never determined why the shooting started.

The shooting, as well as later images of crackdowns on Occupy Wall Street protesters and Black Lives Matter activists, have come to represent the complex and often troubled relationship between

Many citizens are deeply troubled by how law enforcement sometimes responds to protesters, raising concerns about undue force.

armed security personnel and protesters. In too many cases, these forces seem to be at odds, a dynamic that can and has led to violence and death.

Protecting the Rights of All

Protesters are passionate about the causes they advocate and often feel very strongly about their values. But not everyone agrees on what is morally right or wrong, and as a result the protection of the right to protest can also protect the rights of those we don't agree with. Freedom of speech is considered integral to the right to protest, protecting those who voice controversial or minority views from government interference. This has lead to controversial rulings on hate groups, including the KKK and the Westboro Baptist Church, both of which have been found to have a right to protest.

The 1988 Supreme Court case *Boos v. Barry* is one example of a case that defined in some ways how protest and free speech intersect. In that case, the court found that citizens have a right to protest with picket signs outside of foreign embassies and set a precedent that free speech protects public demonstrations that could be called questionable. The precedent has been used to defend a range of protests, and the court itself has cited *Boos v. Barry* when ruling on protest-related cases. In that decision, the court wrote:

> As a general matter, we have indicated that in public debate our own citizens must tolerate insulting, and even outrageous, speech in order to provide adequate breathing space to the freedoms protected by the First Amendment.[2]

Free speech is a right that people passionately defend.

A similarly important, but oftentimes controversial, decision was reached in the 1969 *Brandenburg v. Ohio* case. In that decision, the court found that the KKK had a right to protest without being punished by the government due to inflammatory statements. The decision was controversial because it protects speech in cases other than those in which speech is "directed to inciting or producing imminent lawless action and is likely to incite or produce such action," a vague definition that remains hotly debated today. At protests, where emotions often run high, the line between incitement to violence and merely advocating controversial opinions is much harder to define.

Given the range of issues and causes for which people protest and the strong feelings those who participate have, it can be tempting to differentiate between good and bad protests. But free speech—not to be confused with consequence-free speech— is just as important a cornerstone of our democracy as the freedom to assemble and make our voices heard. As a result, it is crucial that we understand that all protests that are found lawful and safe deserve some level of protection from the state, even if those protesting are voicing opinions with which we do not agree.

Protest Music

Pop culture and protest have been closely linked since the mid-twentieth century, with music at the heart of that relationship. As the Vietnam War raged in the 1960s, folk musicians were on the forefront of recording songs that challenged American power in the world, racism at home, and repressive ideas of society. Some artists, like Woody Guthrie, had been penning protest anthems since the 1930s, but it was in the 1960s that protest music as a genre truly took off in the mainstream. Bob Dylan and Joan Baez, as well as numerous others, rose to fame with songs that were critical of the government, while rock artists like the Beatles and Janis Joplin followed suit shortly thereafter. The Woodstock Music Festival, a famous festival that brought together some of the biggest names in music in 1969, was devoted to a message of love and peace—a message that was critical of the ongoing war in Vietnam. But many feel that celebrity and protest have a complicated relationship, one in

The music of the 1960s often touched on political themes, inspiring young listeners to action. The legendary Woodstock Music Festival, held in 1969, brought many of these musicians together.

which protest and profit are linked. It's something that Neil Young remarked on after the shootings at Kent State when he wrote, "I always felt funny about making money off that. It has never been resolved."[3]

A Historically Controversial Action

Protest has an important and complex place in our civic society. It is at once protected and held sacred, and it is a challenge to the powerful that often becomes controversial. Understanding this dynamic can be confusing, but it is necessary to fully understand protests taking place today or in the future. Inherently political and challenging the status quo, protest has always been about pushing our country forward—in directions with which we may or may not agree. Finding compromises in the wake of protest is a necessary part of governance, but protest itself is meant to spark that change by bringing together like-minded people to send a message to those who are in power. Because of that, it is dangerous, oftentimes radical, and always needed.

The Future of Protest

The history of protest is one of a wave of change that has ebbed and flowed along with our country, and the future of protest is the same. But while we can easily identify the protests that shaped our modern world—from the Boston Tea Party to the suffrage movement to the civil rights movement—it is harder to know what movements taking shape today will be remembered as historic. For every march of millions on the National Mall, there are countless small rallies in communities across the country that influence local affairs in ways that never make the headlines, but they are equally as important as those that are covered in the news.

Protest in all forms, whether it is rallies or petitions, is what keeps our democracy vital and moving forward. It is the ground on which we air our grievances and challenge one another to be better or debate concerns and issues that divide us as a nation. Because of that, protest is a fundamental and crucial piece of our democracy and one that has to be protected and respected by all Americans. Understanding this is necessary for fully understanding the place

White House Peace Vigil

Most protests take place over a day or a few days, featuring events that draw large crowds before parting ways to continue activities in local communities. But some protests last much longer, like the White House Peace Vigil, the longest-running protest in the history of the United States. The vigil began in 1981, when William Thomas set up a stand protesting nuclear weapons directly in front of the White House. Thomas and other activists stayed at the site around the clock, making it a twenty-four-hour-a-day protest. After his death in 2009, Concepcion Picciotto took over, and since her death in 2016, volunteers have manned the tent to ensure it is not removed by authorities. The small construction features signs representing numerous organizations that focus on peace and antiwar and other movements, linking past protest to current issues in a way that has made the site iconic for activists.

The White House Peace Vigil has been active since 1981. Since the death of activist Concepcion Picciotto (*pictured*) in 2016, volunteers have continued the vigil, making it the longest-running protest in US history.

What Does a Protester Do?

As a new generation of young citizens finds its political voice, protest has become more important than ever.

of protest in our history and culture—protesters have never been those who go with the crowd, but rather stand out and stand up for what they believe in. As a result, they are often at odds with those in power. As happened at Kent State, this can mean that authorities dismiss or undermine protesters in ways that are dangerous or that legal challenges to the right to protest can result in an obstruction of the freedom to assemble. It is up to us as citizens to play our part in ensuring lawful protests are respected for what they are—the manifestation of one of our most important civil rights.

The future of protest could look very different from what we know today. Social media has already revolutionized the way we organize and come together, and that role could evolve as organizers find ways to capitalize on the potential of sites like Twitter. But the essence of protest will always be the same, and the power that comes from bringing people together to stand up for something they believe in will always be one of the ways we as a country make progress.

CHAPTER NOTES

Chapter 3: Protecting the Right to Protest

1. "Governor Rhodes Speech on Campus Disorders in Kent, May 3, 1970," Kent State University Library, https://www.library.kent.edu/ksu-may-4-rhodes-speech-may-3-1970.
2. "Boos v. Barry, 485 U.S. 312 (1988)," Justia, https://supreme.justia.com/cases/federal/us/485/312/.
3. Neil Young, *Waging Heavy Peace* (New York, NY: Penguin, 2013).

GLOSSARY

abolitionists Citizens who protested against slavery.

civil disobedience Protesting by breaking minor laws and ordinances, such as curfews or other restrictions, with nonviolent means.

civil rights The rights granted to citizens in order to protect freedom and equality.

counterprotest Protest organized to voice opposition to another existing protest, usually taking place at the same time.

free speech The right to speak without being punished or prosecuted by the government.

governance The act of governing a country.

Jim Crow A system of laws and regulations that imposed racial inequality in post–Civil War southern states, under the slogan "separate but equal."

Magna Carta The first Western document that outlined the rights of citizens, signed in England in 1215.

protester An individual who demonstrates support or opposition to something publicly.

Quakers A religious group that advocates social justice and equality and has a long tradition of protesting injustice.

representation A voice in governance via democratically elected officials.

Seneca Falls Convention A convention of women's rights activists that set out a platform that included the right to vote.

sit-in A form of public protest that involves a group of people going to a specific place and taking up space for a significant amount of time.

Sons of Liberty A guerrilla group of colonial vigilantes who organized protests against British rule.

Stamp Act of 1765 A tax on printed materials imposed by the British on the colonies that sparked widespread protest.

status quo The way things are at any given moment, particularly relating to political or social situations.

Stonewall Riots Spontaneous protests that began at the Stonewall Inn, an LGBTQ+ club in New York City, after an attempted raid by the police; often considered one of the founding moments of the LGBTA+ rights movement of the late twentieth and early twenty-first centuries.

suffrage The right to vote.

Tea Act of 1773 A tax on tea that prompted widespread protest, including the Boston Tea Party, and is considered one of the catalysts for the American Revolution.

FURTHER READING

Books

Artisan. *Why We March: Signs of Protest and Hope—Voices from the Women's March*. New York NY: Artisan, 2017.

Rivera, Sun. *The Dandelion Insurrection*. Santa Cruz, CA: Rising Sun Press Works, 2013.

Tufekci, Zeynep: *Twitter and Tear Gas: The Power and Fragility of Networked Protest*. New Haven, CT: Yale University Press, 2017.

Young, Ralph. *Make Art Not War: Political Protest Posters from the Twentieth Century*. New York, NY: NYU Press, 2016.

Websites

Civil Rights Digital Library
http://crdl.usg.edu/?Welcome
A collection of documents, images, and other information about the fight for civil rights in the United States.

Library of Congress
www.loc.gov
Collection of information and documents about the history of the United States, including protests.

National Archives
www.archives.gov
Collection of information and images about the history of the United States, including protests.

INDEX